FOLK

/ FŌK /

*noun: used as a friendly form
of address to a group of people*

*adjective: of or relating
to the traditional art or culture
of a community*

Quiltfolk

PUBLISHER *Michael McCormick*

EDITOR IN CHIEF *Mary Fons*

CREATIVE DIRECTOR *Janelle Frazier*

MANAGING EDITOR *Jenny Bartoy*

ASSOCIATE EDITOR *Laura McDowell Hopper*

PHOTOGRAPHERS
Azuree Wiitala
Melanie Zacek

CONTRIBUTING WRITERS
Meg Cox
Jenni Grover
Riane Menardi Morrison

GUEST CONTRIBUTORS
American Quilt Study Group
Linda McShannock
Gwen Westerman

Quiltfolk is a community-supported quarterly.
Visit Quiltfolk.com.

SUBMISSIONS
submit@quiltfolk.com

QUESTIONS
hello@quiltfolk.com

/quiltfolk   @quiltfolk   @quiltfolk

PO Box 10796, Eugene, OR 97440
Quiltfolk.com

OPPOSITE: A kit quilt from the collection of scholar Rose Marie Werner is sweet as candy.
PREVIOUS PAGE: Blue patchwork in a quilt designed by Gail Hanson shimmers like a Minnesota lake.

We call this magazine *Quiltfolk* because our content covers two things: quilts and people. The mash-up word "Quiltfolk" is a proper noun when it refers to this publication, but I think lowercase "quiltfolk" has real value too, as in "My guild members are some of the nicest quiltfolk you'll ever meet." For "quiltfolk" to become a real word, however, we're going to need a legitimate definition. What or who are quiltfolk?

I don't believe quiltfolk should include only people who make quilts. I think you're quiltfolk if you collect, repair, catalog, or study quilts. I think you're quiltfolk if you just plain love quilts and respect the people who make them, as in "Billy doesn't know a needle from a bobbin, but he's good quiltfolk just the same." Up until a few months ago, I was happy defining quiltfolk as "people for whom quilts are meaningful in some way."

Then we went to Minnesota.

Minnesota felt blanketed in textiles and textile history of all kinds. We came to explore quilts, and we found those we expected: traditional American, contemporary, and studio-art quilts. But we found other kinds of quilts too: Hmong story cloths and Korean *bojagi*. Beyond the quilts, we came across weavings, crochet, and works of embroidery. Are the people who make and love these textiles quiltfolk too?

When you consider what quiltfolk love about quilts — community, process, heritage, memory, and pretty colors — then these other textile-obsessed people — the knitters, embroiderers, and weavers who care about the exact same things — surely are quiltfolk too.

Without question, quilts and quilters of all kinds will always be at the center of our mission.* But if we open the door just a little and see quilters and their quilts in the larger world of textiles in America, we may find there are a lot more "quiltfolk" around us than we realized.

Welcome to Minnesota, everyone. You're about to meet your kin.

xoxo,

Mary Fons
EDITOR IN CHIEF

*We have dreamed of one day starting *Knitfolk*. Let us know if you're interested!

Quiltfolk

THIS PAGE: A thread rainbow at McTavish Quilting Studio.
ON THE COVER: *Little Women*, made by Nellie Johnson, grandmother of poet-quilter Gwen Westerman, in 1978.
BACK COVER: An interplay of color and geometry in a quilt by Gail Hanson.

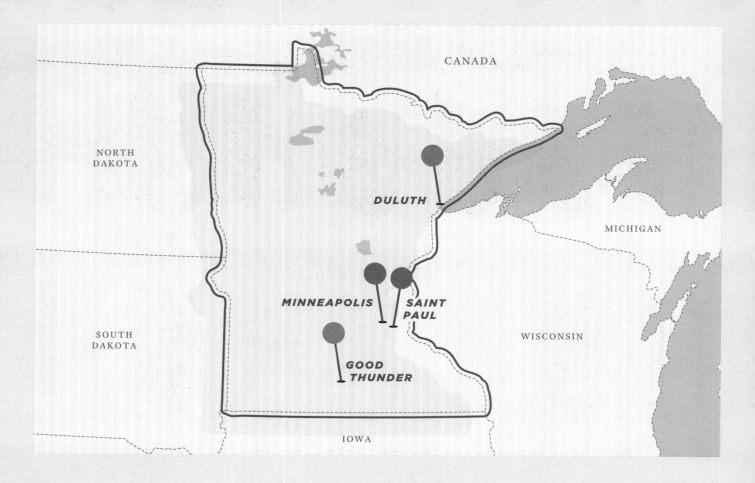

13 | *Minnesota*

You're walking along Duluth's waterfront path on a crisp autumn day. Lake Superior glitters in the sunshine; birds alight on the water. In town, the people — many wearing Vikings jerseys — are just plain nice. You pop into the quilt shop, where everybody knows your name and what quilt you're working on. With your sewing group later that night, you toast and say "Skol!" then enjoy some hot dish — extra tots.

This meditation on the Minnesota good life provides some key impressions of the state. But beyond casseroles and hockey, the Land of 10,000 Lakes is a state with breathtaking natural features: think waterfalls and mountain ranges. The state's most famous city, Minneapolis, is seeing its fastest population growth since the 1950s. The state's populace includes those with heritage from Norway, Southeast Asia, and Somalia as well as Indigenous peoples of the Ojibwe and Dakota tribes. And there aren't 10,000 lakes in Minnesota; it's closer to 12,000.

But why count lakes when you could just sit and sew in a cabin overlooking one? Quilters in Minnesota know how to chill out — yes, especially in winter — and enjoy the good life. For Rose Marie Werner, the good life means studying her favorite topic: vintage quilt kits; for longarm quilter Karen McTavish, it's sharing what she knows; for immigrant Suzanne Thao, the good life in Minnesota means passing on an important appliqué tradition.

What's your idea of the good life? Picture it in your mind — but first, let's see how they do things in Minnesota.

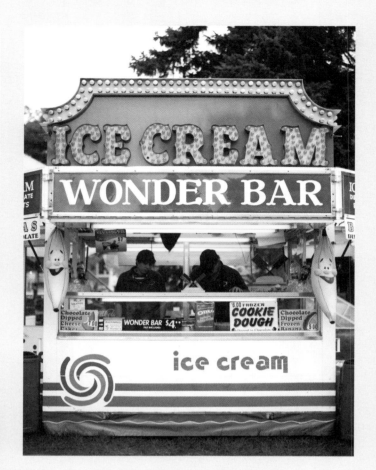

SOUTHERN SKIES

Quilter's Retreat

SOUTHERN SKIES

DUE TO ITS POSITION in the US and its heavenly landscape, Minnesota has been called "the North Star State" — and the nickname fits from the ground up. The southern swath of the state sees a lot of visitors wanting a true Minnesota experience: hiking, fishing, and at least a few hours in charming Midwestern small towns with European roots.

Rochester is the largest city in southern Minnesota and the site of the original Mayo Clinic, the world-renowned hospital founded in 1919.

Down south, there are restaurants that have been in operation since the 1850s, like The Hubbell House in Mantorville (definitely try the cheddar steak). In Walnut Grove, you can visit the childhood home of Laura Ingalls Wilder where quilt patterns are for sale in the gift shop.

Getting to this land of lakes may require flying into Minneapolis. After you collect your luggage, head downstate where southern Minnesota is waiting for you to slow down from your modern pace. Book retreat space with a few quilting friends. Pack your UFOs and some essential staples (like chocolate-chip cookies and wine). Then settle in and enjoy some classic southern Minnesota comfort.

BY **Laura McDowell Hopper**

Gwen Westerman

QUILT POETICS

"I come from a family where there have been quilters for at least six generations who have made quilts from fabric," said Dr. Gwen Westerman. The poet, quilter, and professor does the work of many hands in her century-old farmhouse in Good Thunder, Minnesota, and this includes making quilts connected to her Indigenous heritage.

An enrolled member of the Sisseton Wahpeton Oyate tribe, Westerman has done extensive research on Dakota people and history, enough to know that her ancestors used bone needles and pieced fur for generations before quilting with fabric was introduced in Minnesota by missionaries. This connection to her past informs the quilts Westerman makes in the present, quilts that reference important figures in Dakota history, her tribe's connections to horses and stars, and her family.

Over time, Westerman has blurred the lines between her identities. "There were people who knew me as a professor at the university. There were people who knew me as a poet. And there were people who knew me as a quilt artist," she said. The longer Westerman has been all three, the more this interconnection has enriched her work.

Dr. Gwen Westerman holding her 2009 self-portrait, *From These Hands*.

ABOVE: A paper-pieced test block. OPPOSITE: Westerman and husband Glenn Wasicuna stand for a portrait with Poppy the dog.

Born in Arkansas and raised in Kansas, Westerman finds that quilts are always present in her childhood memories. She remembers sitting on the couch next to her grandmother, staring at the gigantic black-handled scissors her grandmother used to cut individual pieces of fabric and thinking there had to be a faster way to make quilts. Westerman made clothes for her dolls but didn't make her first quilt until she was 40: a baby quilt for a friend having her first child. Westerman moved on to T-shirt quilts, and she also made a Bear Paw quilt for her son, nicknamed Bear, with outlines of their hands as a label. Westerman did not yet know that outlines of her family's hands would become a major theme in her work.

In those early years, she believed that quilts should be functional and large. Watching her grandmother quilt, Westerman had always seen quilts as utilitarian objects, not works of art. "My grandma would never have called herself an artist," Westerman said. Her grandmother worked manual labor jobs by day and quilted at night, a functional pastime while watching TV. When Westerman made quilts as gifts for family, she did not consider herself an artist either. But one publication changed that. A friend offered her an issue of *Quilting Arts Magazine* and as Westerman flipped through the pages, she thought, "I can do this."

Westerman began making art quilts, creating original designs on a small scale and infusing Dakota stories into them. Her color choices and piecing are intricate and seamless, sometimes leading viewers to think her quilts are paintings. Many of her art quilts include a foundation paper-pieced pattern of horses that Westerman drafted herself. "We call them our brothers," Westerman said of horses, "because they carry the burdens that we can't carry."

Wild horses gallop through a wintry scene in Westerman's *Return to Crow Creek*, 2014.

For *Tree of Life*, Westerman used tracings of her grandmother's, mother's, and daughter's hands, as well as her own.

Stars are another recurrent theme for Westerman. "Dakota are star people," she said. In the tribe's creation story, Dakota people originally lived in the stars. Over the years, Westerman had made Star quilts for eight family members and friends. A Star quilt is made by piecing eight colorful diamond wedges; when making each quilt, Westerman crafted an extra diamond with the same fabric. She then pieced the extra diamonds together into a new Star quilt combining the colors and fabrics from the eight previous quilts, along with crystals in the shape of constellations, to connect her family and friends to Dakota knowledge of the stars. That quilt and several others made by Westerman are now in the permanent collection of

the Minnesota History Center, where Westerman was a Native American Artist in Residence.

Westerman started exploring familial themes in her quilts, particularly by including outlines of family members' hands, like she had done in the quilt for her son Bear. In one self-portrait quilt, two hands flank the artist, each holding a needle and stitching. These hands are Westerman's mother's and grandmother's, traced in 2002, the year both women passed away. Westerman held onto the tracings for seven years before finding the emotional energy to use them in a quilt. She chose to create a portrait not only of herself, but also of her mother's and grandmother's hands appearing to sew her into existence, with her father looking down at them from the stars.

Westerman's focus on hands in her quilts emphasizes that her quilts are handmade and connects her through time to artists whose hand outlines date back to rock art. She also explores the way that passing generations will lose knowledge of the ancestors' hands over time. "I held my grandma's hand, my children held my grandma's hand," Westerman said. "But anybody who comes after them won't have that connection." By preserving her family's hands in her quilts, Westerman is ensuring that future generations will be able to see and touch their ancestors' hands.

As her art quilt career flourished, the lines between Westerman's academic, poet, and quilter identities began to blur. One of her quilts was used for the cover of her book *Mni Sota Makoce: The Land of the Dakota*, a collaborative history tome about Dakota relationships to the land in Minnesota. Quilts have also crept into Westerman's poetry. Her 2013 collection *Follow the Blackbirds* centers on the theme of coming home and includes frequent sewing imagery and themes. "When I thought about home, quilts have been part of my life for as long as I can remember," Westerman said. The quilting themes were not intentional, but images of her family's quilts came to her time and time again as she was writing. "I think it's two sides of the same coin for me to be a poet and a quilter, because you're taking little things — words or pieces of fabric — and putting them together to make a picture."

Westerman continues to research and teach others about Dakota history and culture. She's currently working on the first volume of a book about letters written by Dakota teachers between 1835 and 1875, a period of time where Indigenous peoples in America were forcibly removed en masse from their ancestral and rightful lands.

Through her quilts, she also hopes to teach about Dakota people and their persistence, especially in Minnesota. "We are still here," Westerman said. "We are in every occupation imaginable. We still have strong connections to this land. Our language marks this land. We are teachers, and police officers, and air traffic controllers, and your next-door neighbor." And a poet and professor, making quilts in her farmhouse studio. Ⓠ

TOP: Letters written in Dakota language in the 19th century have sparked a research project. **BOTTOM:** A dream catcher in the artist's sewing room. **OPPOSITE:** *Little Women*, 1978, made by Westerman's grandmother, Nellie Johnson.

A fabric landscape takes shape on the poet's design wall.

Quilt Label

By Gwen Westerman

If
we
follow a pattern, a path, a river,
flowing like a current of memory
cell-deep, like migratory birds intent on
returning to and returning from the places where they
were born, among wetlands and wild rice, glacial lakes and maple groves,
we may remember how it feels to float along a river at the edge of a dream.
Stories of family lost, of families yet to form, trace patterns of generations of hands
cutting, pinning, piecing, reaching backward and forward from the places where they were born.
No words fasten the thoughts in a stitch, a thousand stitches, ten thousand stitches. Would we start
down that path if we knew the final number? Who will count our stitches, touch what we
touched, stroke the grain of the fabric, hold it up to the light, and wonder what we
were thinking in the dead of winter when we took the first stitch? We were
thinking of the headwaters of the Mississippi, where we stood in water
so clear yet so shallow it barely covered our feet, of Lake Superior
where it lapped at the North Shore and caressed agates and
whispered sweet dreams of stars, of our grandmothers' laps
and working-class hands. We were thinking of prairies and
grasslands rolling green and gold for as far as we could see,
of running with the wind atop the ridge, of mussel shells
and beaver dams along the Maple River, of our children's
first breaths, reimagining the past in the present where
the Minnesota bends northward, of the stitches that
bind us together, like an appliquéd hand holding a
heart. We were thinking of bluebirds as they sang
in the maples and black willows along the Cannon,
its currents rolling among the bluffs toward
the sea. A thousand words cannot convey those
thoughts, those hopes and memories carried in
our stitches, each one an adoration of the stories
reimagined by our hands. Connecting water to
land and sky to stars, we dream as we stitch
the past to the future, the unseen to the unknown,
knowing we are not alone as long as we have a map
to follow, a song to sing. Even if we knew the final number,
if we knew there would be no one to count our stitches, we would
do it all again, blanketed in the warmth of those pieces as they weave
stories into patterns. We would thread that first needle, connect land
to water, winter to spring, a tenderly composed desire to be remembered,
and with the last caress bind ourselves to the edges of an unseen well of faith.
We would tie the knot and sign the label. "Stitched with love, Minnesota 2019."

BY **Meg Cox**

The Kit Is All Right
ROSE MARIE WERNER

The life of Rose Marie "Rosie" Werner, a farm girl and former nun, has been marked by passion. Unexpected passion.

Werner put on a habit right out of high school and soon started a somewhat itinerant life as a grade-school teacher. Her religious order sent her to small Minnesota towns to teach mostly immigrant children and she lived in the local convents. After 14 years, the lifestyle wore Werner down and she left the order. "I transferred so many times, I never felt like I belonged anywhere," she said.

For four years, Werner lived alone and worked as a religious educator. Then at age 35, she discovered where she belonged: with farmer Eugene Werner. The love of her life stood 14 inches taller than her 5-foot frame and called himself her "off-white knight" because, he said, he wasn't perfect.

Rosie Werner settled into the Werner family farm in tiny Dundas, Minnesota. She became a mother of three and bookkeeper for the family seed business, delving into every passing craft in her spare time. She decided in the 1990s that she derived the greatest satisfaction from quilting. But about 15 years ago, she discovered the second unexpected love of her life: quilt kits.

Rose Marie Werner shows off a *Star of the East* patch from a 1932 quilt kit.

ABOVE: Evidence of an avid quilter. **OPPOSITE:** When Werner's husband Eugene built her sewing table, he taped a sign to the top: "Make It Amazing." **NEXT PAGE:** Detail, *Wedgewood*, an unfinished 1943 kit quilt that Werner hand quilted herself.

"I have to admit that I was a bit of a snob about quilt kits. I saw them as being less desirable because they were not the original designs of the makers," Werner said. She explained that quilt kits are "commercial packages that include fabric components for a quilt top and some sort of printed, predetermined pattern to be appliquéd or embroidered or quilted."

Werner stood in a spare bedroom, near a bed piled high with vintage quilts, many with white backgrounds appliquéd with brightly colored flower motifs in the centers and borders. Behind her were an open cupboard and closet stuffed with stacks of additional quilts, most of them also made with the finest of workmanship — from quilt kits.

Werner's sentiments about quilts made from kits were (and still are) pretty common. Kit quilts are the Rodney Dangerfields of the quilt world: They get no respect. Quilt historian Merikay Waldvogel said, "For ages, everybody was mostly interested in 19th-century quilts. Those were the glory days." By comparison, quilts from the mid-20th century were considered more pedestrian and kit quilts were literally shunned, derided as the quilting equivalent of paint-by-number paintings.

ABOVE: Embroidered blocks in this *Tabby's Day* kit design from W. L. M. Clark Inc. depict a day in the life of a kitten. **OPPOSITE:** Werner holds a crib quilt called *Bunny Hop*, first "kitted" in 1967.

Quilt kits came in various configurations but generally contained precut pieces to save time. The die-cut pieces might have been diamonds or other shapes meant for a pieced top, or shapes like butterflies meant for appliqué. Appliqué kits, which were especially popular, often included large pieces of white background fabric stamped with blue sewing lines to indicate placement. Fabric for flowers, vines, or other shapes would also be marked and numbered so quilters could easily place the pieces on the background and stitch them down.

In the late 1990s, when the International Quilt Museum in Lincoln, Nebraska, started working with the large collection of quilts donated by collectors Ardis and Robert James, curators were surprised to discover that about 80 quilts, roughly 10 percent of the total given to the museum, had been made from period kits. Quilt scholar Virginia Gunn was examining the quilts, said Carolyn Ducey, now curator of collections, and "she started to point at different quilts and say, 'This is a kit. This is a kit. Did you know this one was a kit?' I was completely blown away." The story reminds Ducey how little was known about kit quilts 30 years ago.

But many of these quilts were well designed and masterfully sewn, and experts began to reconsider the genre. "To finish one of those quilt kits was a major accomplishment," said Waldvogel. "They were marketed as easy and efficient, but some had hundreds of pieces. You had to be an excellent seamstress."

Lillian Walker of Iowa created this dazzling *Bird Lover's Guide* design in the mid-1950s. Her kits arrived with basted pieces for the purchaser to appliqué.

Experts were led to reconsider kit quilts partly due to a 2003 exhibition in Lincoln called *Modern Marvels: Quilts Made from Kits, 1915-1950*. Curator Deborah Rake explained that kits were embraced as cool, modern shortcuts that suited the times. "After all, during this era Sears & Roebuck [*sic*] was offering kits to build houses," she wrote. Today's quilters, whose studios are full of precut fabrics and tools like rotary cutters and longarm quilting machines, can certainly understand the impulse for efficiency.

The *Modern Marvels* show rocked Rosie Werner's world. "In the gallery [I saw] one gorgeous quilt after another, beautifully appliquéd or pieced and quilted," she said, so she changed her mind about kits. "Suddenly I wanted to document them, see how many designers and styles there were. I was hooked."

Thus began a 13-year endeavor during which Werner produced an extensive website documenting more than 4,000 designs produced by some 40 companies. She studied the work of designers like Marie Webster, "the first quilt celebrity in America," who produced kits as early as 1915, and Ruby McKim, whose embroidered quilt-block designs were published in newspapers all over the country. McKim sold her popular patterns and kits through a catalog she published with her husband. Werner discovered that some companies like Bucilla who sold high-end sewing supplies got into the kit business partly to sell more embroidery floss. Their kit fabrics were stamped for appliqué designs meant to be supplemented by embroidery.

ABOVE: Quilts from Werner's collection: a lilac *May Day Basket* design by Hubert Ver Mehren and a floral appliqué of unknown origin.
OPPOSITE: When making her own quilts, Werner doesn't necessarily require a kit.

Werner's work has been so well received that appraisers, historians, and curators are willing to pay $40 subscriptions to search her archives at QuiltKitID.com. Recently, she self-published a critically lauded book, *Quilt Kits: 20th Century Short Cuts*. "For years, I felt I was standing on the shoulders of others who studied this before me, but after 13 years, I started seeing trends and having opinions, so I decided to write the book," said Werner.

Historians like Waldvogel who have been studying kits and the quilts made from them for decades are impressed by how much Rosie Werner has added to the available knowledge. "She is a true collector in this niche area and has really made a name for herself. Rosie is humble, hard-working, and determined: a great-hearted woman."

If you ask Werner, she'll tell you that unexpected passion pays off. Her other great love — husband Eugene — continues to bring her joy, as their marriage enters its 45th year.

THE TWIN CITIES

Stitched Together

THE TWIN CITIES

IT MAKES SENSE that two facing cities would attract quilters. We're all about "facing" fabrics together, after all.

Sitting opposite each other on a narrow stretch of the Mississippi River, Saint Paul and Minneapolis were given the nickname "Twin Cities" in the 19th century. Each city has its own mayor and government, but Minneapolis and Saint Paul are happy siblings, sharing traditions and culture among their combined population of 3.25 million. On both sides of the river you'll find museums, nightlife, folk festivals, a vibrant music scene, plus a lot of Twin Cities pride.

If pop superstar Prince made Minneapolis his home for most of his life, it's got to be cool. The quilt scene in the Twin Cities is cool too. In the metro area, some guilds have been meeting for more than 40 years, and the relatively newer Minneapolis Modern Quilt Guild just celebrated its 10th anniversary. In a metropolis this big, you'll find your people — and we're more than happy to begin the introductions. You're about to meet talented quilt "kween" Arianna Caggiano, a modern-style quilter who has made her charming home and thriving business in Saint Paul. And in Minneapolis, the staff at Textile Center is ready to share their current class schedule.

See? You've already got quilt friends in not just one city, but two.

BY **Riane Menardi Morrison**

Arianna Caggiano
THE QUILT KWEEN

A pennant proclaiming the trendy catchphrase "Yas Queen" hangs on the wall of Arianna Caggiano's sunroom.

The space was sprinkled with newly minted QuiltKween originals: brightly colored pillows with graphic patterns, modern improvisational patchwork, and appliquéd eggs (yes, fried eggs). On her floor were neatly organized tubs full of pouches with minimal stripes, scrappy half-square triangles, chunky zippers, and avocado-print linings. Her signature QuiltKween labels put the final, sophisticated touch on goods that would be sold at Porter Flea, a show in Nashville that she'd drive 14 hours to attend as a vendor — and she was leaving in two days. "I'm on like, two hours of sleep right now," Caggiano said. "It's been a wild few weeks."

Millennial quilter makes good: Arianna Caggiano in her sunroom.

ABOVE, L-R: Sammich the dog makes frequent appearances on Caggiano's Instagram feed; a portrait of Sammich created by friend Jackie Peetz in 2017. **OPPOSITE:** Free-range lines, intelligently pieced.

When we met Arianna Caggiano on a muggy June morning, she had recently moved cross-country from Savannah, Georgia. The movers came on her 29th birthday. She's now settled in her new home with faithful companion Sammich, a furry black dog with a mustard-yellow bandanna, who shuffled at her feet, blending into her color scheme as seamlessly as if he were one of her quilts. Wall hangings were slung temporarily in her dining room (they'd soon be packed up for the show), displaying the level of finesse you'd expect from an art school grad: leading lines, thoughtful details, and an eye for balance and composition.

Caggiano's work is the product of 10 years of quilting, including a stint at the Savannah College of Art and Design (SCAD) where she studied fiber arts and learned the art and business of quilting. After college, Caggiano worked as a textile designer for Kohl's for five years. During that time, she lost her brother to bacterial meningitis. "I didn't really dive into my style until [then,] using quilting as a way to heal and distract myself," she said.

In 2017, Caggiano turned her gaze toward her QuiltKween business full-time. Her work shifts effortlessly from precision-pieced to free-form to whimsical, and her creative voice screams fresh, stylish, and fun.

Caggiano is part of the new generation of artisans redefining the business of quilting. She's scrappy (in both the material and business senses), with an art student's eye, a millennial's drive, and an entrepreneur's business savvy. She developed her voice over years of practice and experimentation and honed her business chops through trial and error.

ABOVE: Trinkets and objets d'art spark memories and ideas. **OPPOSITE:** QuiltKween inventory awaits shipping.

As a SCAD student, Caggiano was trained to blend art and business and she learned from some of the best, like Pamela Wiley, her longtime quilt and textile professor and mentor. "I was honestly spoiled with the amount of time I had with her," Caggiano said. "She's one of the most incredible professors I've ever had and one of the most influential people in my life. She taught us to do what you love and love what you do, and you'll eventually find somebody who will pay you to do it. I love that idea."

Caggiano's drive to do what she loves has paid off. Her distinctive style has earned her tens of thousands of Instagram followers, and she continues to inspire and push boundaries. "I think the best way to take risks in quilting is by working small," she said. "A lot of people try to start with a queen-size quilt, when in reality they should be trying new fabrics, new batting, different materials and just seeing what clicks. It's bound to evolve if you just keep pushing."

In her own work, Caggiano also looks to art, graphic design, and architecture for inspiration, reinterpreting elements, composition, and balance into her quilts. Her totes and wall hangings evoke the lines of modern buildings, and the abstract grids in her work bring to mind digital design. "There's so much to quilting. It's so unlimited to me, the idea of it," she said. "You can experiment and go wild with it." Caggiano says one of the things that inspires her most about quilting is pushing the idea of what quilts can be and what others perceive them to be.

ABOVE: Prepped components of zipper pouches. **OPPOSITE:** The artist, her sketchbook, and a big design wall.

Caggiano has reached a point where she "loves the pigeonhole I'm in," she said, and every piece of work personifies her creative voice. As she showed us around her studio, her energy was as cool and confident as her work. Her space exudes the perfect middle ground between organization and creative chaos. The walls are covered with art made by her and others. In her sketchbook, broken needles are taped next to early versions of her logo.

Caggiano designs her own fabrics featuring hand-drawn egg and avocado motifs, and she looks at her work with an artist's eye — confident in what she creates but distant. She's quick to point out the joins and repeats in her fabric, for instance. But she says being detached from her work helps. "I'm able to create a lot more work, and I don't really mind if it sells or if it doesn't sell, you know?"

Caggiano's laser focus and hard work have helped put her on the map in the last few years. In 2019, she was invited to be part of Madewell's Hometown Heroes Collective and sell a collection of pillows and wall hangings on madewell.com. In 2018, she was selected for Craftsy's Quilt Designer Fellowship, then she released quilt patterns and kits with the company (rebranded as Bluprint) in fall of 2019. She also sells handmade quilted goods at national craft fairs and has a hard time keeping her most popular items in stock.

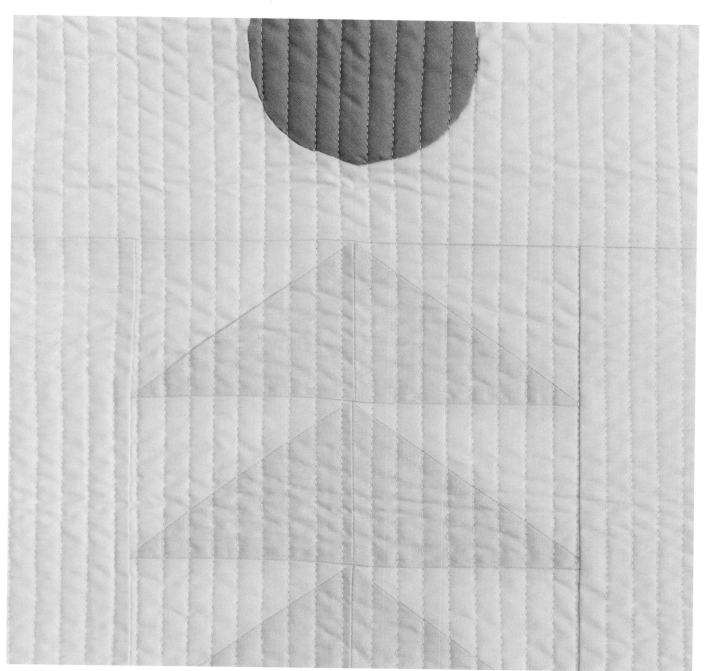

ABOVE: Straight-line quilting and solid fabrics are hallmarks of the modern quilt style. **OPPOSITE:** A sun-drenched back porch was a big selling point when Caggiano was house-hunting.

ABOVE: A signature palette: burnt umber, deep teal, and mustard yellow play well together. OPPOSITE: Caggiano takes a moment for the camera before getting back to work.

Caggiano sees quilts — especially modern quilts — making their way into the mainstream. "People think quilting is a dying craft, and I'm like, 'Where did you get that idea?'" she said. "I feel like it's in its renaissance stage. There's so much more diversity and there's so much more innovation in the quilting world now than ever before."

The next phase of QuiltKween is focused on making patterns and leading workshops to teach and inspire the next generation of quilters. Caggiano believes the idea of making is powerful. "I feel like there's something impermanent about the technological world," she said. "You can lose whatever is on your hard drive, but if you make a quilt, it's forever. There's something really valuable to me about that, actually making something with your hands."

Evolution is in Caggiano's nature. As her brand, business, and creative voice continue to push the boundaries, dedication remains the driving force. "It's a lot of work. It's a lot of tears. But I love making, and I love quilting, and there are more good days than bad. It is really stressful, but it's definitely worth it."

BY **Meg Cox**

Linda McShannock

AT THE MINNESOTA HISTORY CENTER

It takes all sorts of objects, both grand and humble, to tell the story of a state through its history museum. Minnesota is known for lakes and prairies and for the furs and grain mills that built its economy. But quilts are part of that history too, explained Textile Curator Linda McShannock. At the Minnesota History Center in Saint Paul, McShannock shared what the 400-plus quilts in the collection say about her state.

The Minnesota History Center collection includes prizewinning quilts from the Minnesota State Fair *(see page 72)*; Native American quilts made by Dakota and Ojibwe artists; and a good selection of quilts brought here by Scandinavian, German, and Irish immigrants and Easterners, who moved west in the mid-19th century to work in mills and mines. In addition, the Center boasts more than 300 examples of embroidered textiles by a more recent immigrant group, the Hmong people *(see page 104)*.

Curator Linda McShannock, an advocate for quilts and textiles everywhere — especially those in Minnesota.

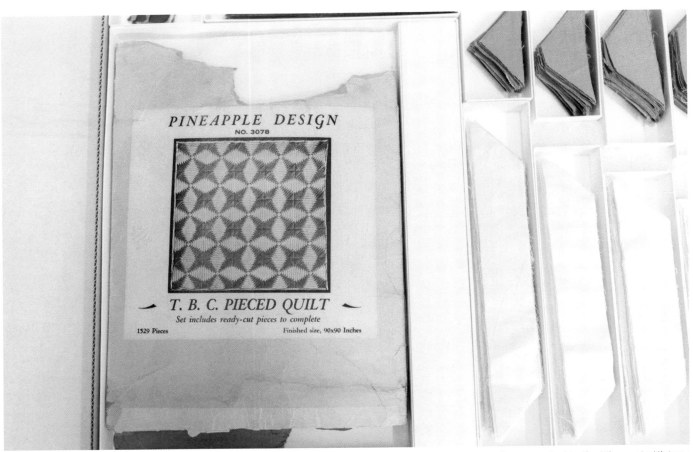

PINEAPPLE DESIGN
NO. 3078

T. B. C. PIECED QUILT

Set includes ready-cut pieces to complete

1529 Pieces   Finished size, 90x90 Inches

ABOVE: A vintage quilt kit is preserved in the collections room. **OPPOSITE:** McShannock feels personally connected to the Minnesota History Center's textile holdings. **NEXT PAGE:** The makers of this 18th-century quilt from Norway worked with sumptuous silk taffeta.

"I think of this as my room," Linda McShannock said as she unlocked the door to a cavernous space filled with 10-foot-tall steel storage cabinets arranged in rows. "This room houses about 25,000 textile and clothing items. When I want to bond with the collection, this is where I stand and just open drawers. Those are my pieces: I know their stories." During a quarter of a century working as a curator for the Minnesota Historical Society, which runs the Center, McShannock has handled, hung, researched, and repaired thousands of objects.

The first quilt she laid out on a table was a shimmering apple-green whole-cloth quilt made of woven silk in the late 18th century in Norway. The fine hand-quilted design includes an intricate rose encircled with scrolls and shells. Other floral motifs include tulips and a flowering vine in the borders. Not only is this 200-year-old quilt in immaculate condition, but its story has fascinated the curator for decades. "This quilt was donated to us in the 1960s," McShannock explained, but "lore has it that the quilt was brought to America in 1882 and passed down through five generations."

This treasured silk quilt was made by three sisters in Bergen, Norway — one of whom became the grandmother of a famous Norwegian, Ole Bull. Bull was a celebrated violinist and composer who started a short-lived utopian community for Norwegian immigrants in Pennsylvania and promoted Norwegian culture through his life. Today Minnesota boasts close to a million Norwegian Americans and one statue of Bull, a violin tucked under his chin, in a Minneapolis park.

The green quilt exerts a pull on the curator partly because the makers' descendants used to come visit their heirloom on a regular basis. "I would open the quilt and unroll it and all of us would stand in a circle and hear the story from the matriarch," said McShannock. "The quilt is their connection to Norway and it gave me goose bumps every time."

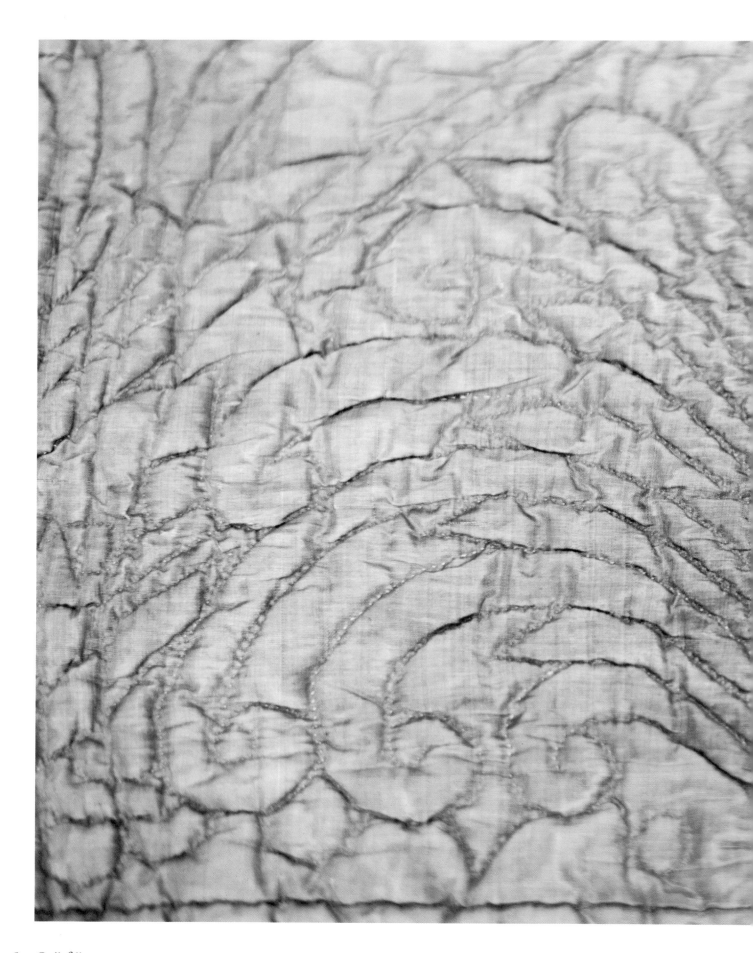

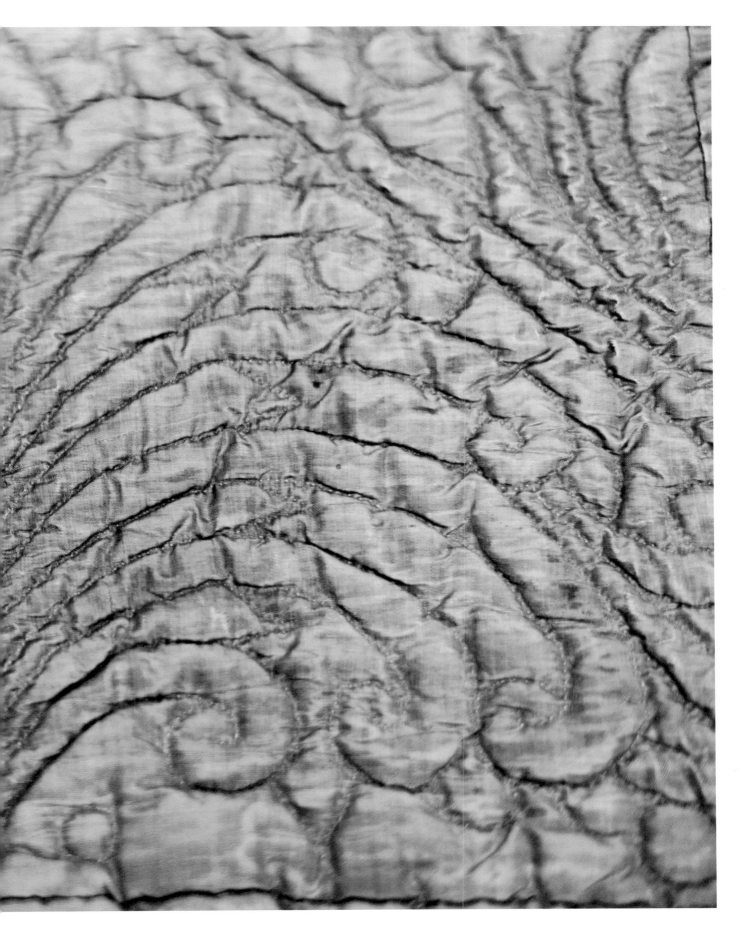

CLOCKWISE FROM UPPER LEFT: McShannock's favorites in the collection include *Motherwort* (detail) by Clare Degerness; *Caske's Pardon* by Gwen Westerman; and Minnesota artist Erica Spitzer Rasmussen's *Earl Grey's Quilt*.

Curious about textiles of all kinds, McShannock created this experimental needle felting at a friend's "studio play day."

Tracking down the history of quilts is part of what keeps McShannock excited about her work. But her passion isn't purely for the past. She wants the collection to illustrate and illuminate the story of quilts and quilters in Minnesota up to the present.

Another quilt she brought out to share was *Earl Grey's Quilt*, made by local artist Erica Spitzer Rasmussen in 1999. The quilt's title refers to the chief material in the piece: used tea bags. The square bags, still full of dried tea which have stained them in mottled shades of brown, tan, and taupe, have been stitched together and backed with paper.

"This is the biggest risk I ever took as a curator," said McShannock about asking the museum to acquire something that will be tricky to conserve and isn't, strictly speaking, a quilt. "It may self-destruct, but we'll keep it as long as we can." McShannock believes the artwork makes a statement about how the idiom of quilting is being interpreted by contemporary artists.

Though she doesn't quilt, McShannock is a multimedia crafter and seamstress, proud to point out that she made the striking black-and-white vest she wore that day. "I'm happy being a dabbler," she said. "I like to explore many textile traditions with my own hands. I learned to spin and to tat. I knit, do needle felting and hand stitching, and I especially love to dye with natural resources like berries and bark." And every stitch she takes, every dye she brews increase Linda McShannock's appreciation for the wide range of textiles under her care.

Jason Onerheim

Assistant Collections Manager Jason Onerheim is in charge of documenting every object that comes into the Minnesota Historical Society — including the quilts.

Museums and publications like *Quiltfolk* use "flat shots" of quilts. Any quilt contest requires a flat shot of the entry. What's a flat shot?
A flat shot is a photograph of a whole quilt. Here, that's done by either hanging it, laying it flat, or placing it on a slant board.

How do you decide which method to use?
The first step is to assess the condition: Can this quilt be moved easily? Can it be handled without causing damage? If a quilt has been shown before, it will often have a sleeve, sometimes put on by the quilter, or it might have a strip of velcro sewn in by a conservator. That means I can hang the quilt for the photo. If not, it goes on a slant board.

What happens if the textile can't be moved easily, because it's really old or delicate? Most people would be afraid to breathe on a quilt like that.
It is very nerve-wracking, but I can ask our textile curator for assistance. And I'm a strange museum photographer: most of my experience working in museums is in art handling, installation, and registrarial work. This makes me a one-stop shop because I can handle the artifact *and* photograph it.

Tell us why you turned the lights off for some pictures and kept them on for others.

For the full flat shot, I want the lighting to be as even as possible, so I use four lights. But when you have such even lighting, it's hard to see the quilting or any 3-D aspects of the quilt. To get that, I use what's called "raking light" where you use just one or two lights. That lighting brings out the detail.

This studio is huge, but there are some monster quilts out there. What's the biggest quilt you've photographed?

The largest flat shot I took was a Minnesota State Fair quilt from 1968, which came in at 114 by 100 inches. When a quilt is that big, I sometimes take four separate pictures and then "stitch" them together in the computer.

"Stitch" them together? Nice one! Thanks, Jason. 🇶

The quilt photographed in this story is *October's Misty Morn*, made in 1991 by Eunice Hill of Minnesota.

BY **Jenni Grover**

Best in Show

MINNESOTA STATE FAIR

———————

Every summer more than two million fairgoers flock from around the state to attend "The Great Minnesota Get-Together." They wander the 322-acre fair grounds to ride the Great Big Wheel, marvel at beautiful crafts, and maybe catch the 4-H Lama Costume Competition. Scattered throughout the fair, vendors sell nearly 500 foods, many served on a stick. (New offerings this year included the Deep-Fried Dilly Dog, a pickle stuffed with bratwurst, dipped in batter, and fried.)

Not to be outdone, the fair's Creative Activities Building for the past six years has exhibited "Quilts on a Stick," a competition of tiny quilts that often poke fun at fair traditions. This year's theme was "Have you ever seen a cow dance?" It was just one of 25 categories of award-winning quilts displayed at the Minnesota State Fair in 2019.

Browsing the show's 300 quilts on display in the Creative Activities Building, you get a feel for what makes a winner: crisp mitered corners, smart color choices, precise stitches. For even more insight into what makes an award-winning quilt, *Quiltfolk* caught up with this year's judge and a handful of previous blue-ribbon winners.

The Minnesota State Fair is fun for kids of all ages — and quilters too.

ABOVE, L-R: Judge David Shattuck samples fare from the fair; ribbons are nice, but the quilters say enjoyment in quiltmaking matters most.
OPPOSITE: *Pronto* is a textile topiary created for the fair by the Minnesota Knitters' Guild.

The judge

Traditional quilter David Shattuck has served as a needlecraft competition judge since 1995, alternating years with another person. While he expects mastery of the craft, perfection isn't his top priority when judging quilts. "I know that not every point will be perfect, not every seam will be straight," he said. He rewards quilters for taking risks with skill and offers constructive criticism on the feedback cards, explaining why a quilter fell short of a perfect score of 100. "We're Minnesota nice. I do 80s and 90s generally. Very few 70s."

Shattuck says many quilters falter in the final steps of their quilts. "Binding is the least understood technique, and the one technique that [quilters] want to get over with as quickly as possible." He grew animated as he listed the ways binding could be improved. He expects nicely mitered corners and a short, tight stitch for tacking binding to the back. And the binding join? Don't get him started. "Too many quilters tuck it under and stitch it down, and you end up with a large, thick knot," he said.

Motivations for entering quilts in the state fair vary, from quilters who are driven to win to folks who just want friends and family to see their creations on display. No matter the reason, Shattuck said, quilters can learn a lot from the experience.

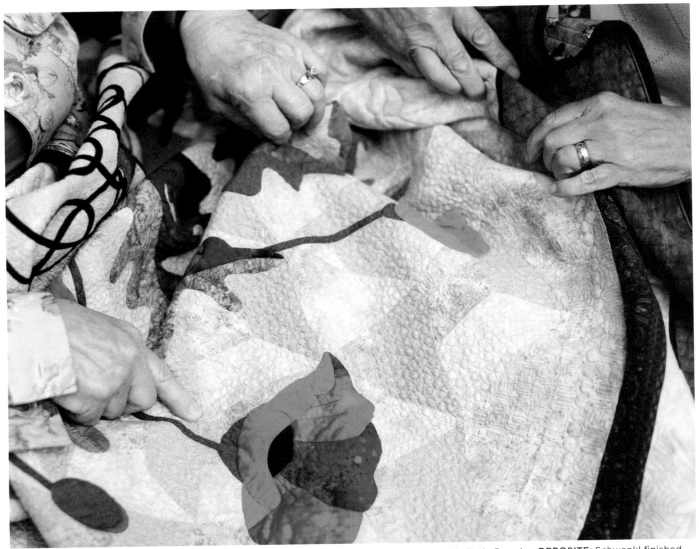

ABOVE: Masterful appliqué blooms from a low-volume background in Carol Schwankl's *Celtic Patio Poppies*. **OPPOSITE:** Schwankl finished this particular masterpiece in 2007.

Beautifully satisfying

Carol Schwankl makes traditional quilts with machine piecing and hand appliqué, quilting by hand and machine. A member of four local guilds, she savors the connections she makes with other quilters, especially the friends who offer honest feedback, which she treasures as a way to learn and improve.

As we sat together, Schwankl and friend Victoria Miller compared notes on techniques. Schwankl listed her main goals: "All the points are there. Appliqué edges are turned under well. The quilting is elaborate and appropriate." Schwankl is so careful to perfect every detail that she once quilted an entire project but, unsatisfied with the results, ripped it out stitch by stitch to start over again.

She doesn't enter quilts every year but when she does, she often wins, usually in categories that celebrate a combination of techniques like appliqué and machine piecing. She favors traditional color palettes (the quilt she showed us was covered in bold shades of green and red) and texture-adding techniques like tiny stippling and trapunto. She's won Sweepstakes — the top prize at the fair — three times. "There is so much satisfaction in being able to create a piece of beauty," Schwankl said. "So long as my hands are capable, I will be quilting."

ABOVE: The palette of her blue-ribbon quilt matches Mary Alsop's colorful style. **OPPOSITE:** *Paradox Point* was also a winner in the Modern category at the 2018 Minnesota Quilters' Show.

A cheerleader for quilters

Mary Alsop is modest about her winning quilts. "I always think I can improve," she said, even though she has won awards for both her piecing and her quilting. She seeks out ways to keep learning, and competing at the fair provides her with helpful feedback.

Alsop thinks many quilters are overly self-critical, which keeps them from entering quilts in the fair. A longarm quilter, Alsop said some of her clients shy away from entering, so each year she sends them letters encouraging them to compete. The letters act as a creative prod that motivates her clients to enter and motivates *her* to keep doing incredible work for them. Many of her clients have won prizes.

Alsop's ribbons hang in her longarm room, a validation she can see each day as she works. The ribbons are a reminder that her work is respected. "I don't have to be so critical of myself."

On her 2019 Sweepstakes-winning quilt, Alsop combined a variety of techniques and melded traditional and contemporary quilting motifs. Not one to rest on her laurels, she said she'll continue to up her game by taking classes from renowned teachers and learning from judges' critiques.

ABOVE: Victoria Miller demonstrates exquisite hand quilting in *Mrs. Brown's Lovely Daughter*, 2010. **OPPOSITE:** Every component of Miller's design is thoughtfully sewn.

Hours well spent

Victoria Miller has been entering quilts at the state fair since 1990. But not every year. She usually makes just one quilt every couple of years, spending countless hours on traditional needle-turn appliqué and hand quilting. She loves quilts that honor traditional styles, like the Baltimore Album which originated in the 1840s, and that feature classic color combinations of bright reds, crisp greens, and soothing browns. She has won a ribbon every time she has entered a quilt in the competition.

In addition to county- and state-level awards,

Miller has also won the prized Bill and Helen Kelley Memorial Award for hand quilting five times. Helen Kelley was a Minnesotan, a member of The Quilters Hall of Fame, and a beloved columnist for *Quilters Newsletter* magazine.

Miller has collected enough ribbons to fill two boxes. "You would think the thrill would be gone, but it isn't!" she said. Miller didn't have a quilt in the 2019 Minnesota State Fair, but that's okay. She's content to work steadily, at home in her favorite chair.

ABOVE: A quilter who works in many styles, Nancy Birger holds her mini quilt *Haboob*, 2015. **OPPOSITE:** Birger took top prize with *Carol's Appliqué* in 2014.

The controversial technique

Nancy Birger doesn't usually set out to make a quilt to show at the fair. "As I've gotten older, I've become a little more casual and a little more careless," she said, "because to me, it's what I'm making and who I'm giving it to that's important." That might mean she sews on her binding with a machine instead of hand finishing it, for example. And if it wins a prize at the fair? "That's nice."

But don't think that means Birger's quilts aren't works of art. In 25 years of entering state fairs, she has won many awards. Her 2019 blue-ribbon winner, *Bighorn Sheep*, is a pictorial study in raw-edge appliqué. "Things like this are always very controversial, because they're appliqué but not traditional appliqué," said Birger.

In the past, a rumor spread that judge Shattuck's traditional style meant he didn't like raw-edge appliqué. But "I can appreciate raw-edge — I just like to see it well-done," he said. Birger joked with Shattuck and quipped: "I got yelled at one year because I entered two quilts in the same category, and [Shattuck] said he couldn't give them both a blue ribbon." That's a problem most quilters would like to have.

ABOVE: All's "fair" in quilts and community. L-R: Birger, Alsop, Miller, Andrea Salisbury, Schwankl. **OPPOSITE:** Salisbury admits her 2015 ribbon winner, *Tomato Stars*, is a personal favorite.

A chance to learn

Andrea Salisbury has been quilting since she was 18, but she has only ever entered one quilt at the state fair. For years, she thought the judges were looking for perfection, which felt unattainable. "I'm always just trying to make, so I'm not as focused on the 'perfect' part," she said.

Then Salisbury showed her quilt *Tomato Stars* at a meeting of the Minneapolis Modern Quilt Guild, and friends urged her to enter it in the state fair. *Tomato Stars* won a blue ribbon in 2015.

Today, Salisbury feels like the state fair quilt competition is anybody's game. "They're looking for perfection, but they're also looking for the intangibles, like is it pleasing to the eye?" she explained. "And that's going to be different for everyone."

Salisbury thinks the judges' feedback is one of the best things about entering shows. "If you don't take it personally," she said, "the judges really do give you a lot of good insights that your friends will not."

BY **Meg Cox**

Act One

QUILTS AT PENUMBRA THEATRE

Theaters are a place of magic. Theaters unfold stories that heal, teach, and enrapture. Penumbra Theatre in Saint Paul has been unfolding stories about the African American experience since 1976 and sometimes, those tales are best told with quilts.

Take the iconic black playwright August Wilson's *Gem of the Ocean*, a play about the dark roots of slavery. The mystical central character, Aunt Ester, possesses a quilt that she says is a map to the City of Bones, a spiritual place under the ocean made from the bones of enslaved Africans who died on ships traveling to the New World. When mounting a production of *Gem* in 2008, Penumbra reached out to local quilter Cecile Margaret Lewis to make Aunt Ester's quilt for the play. Her haunting masterpiece turned out to be far more than a prop.

Cecile Margaret Lewis with the quilt she designed for *Black Nativity* in 2010.

Lewis and fellow quilter Gail Hanson talk quilts and plays.

"I decided to use the Storm at Sea block" throughout the quilt, Lewis told the *Quiltfolk* crew as she sat in the 135-seat theater. The shades of blue in her blocks gradually transform into bleached-out white linen at the quilt's center, representing the bones of the dead. Lewis said it was harrowing to make. To represent lost souls, some patches within the blocks are grey, while others that represent survivors are brown. Today, the quilt is framed and hanging in the Penumbra lobby.

Lewis, a gregarious woman whose figure might be called willowy but for the strength she exudes, also talked about a longer-lived quilt connection she had with Penumbra around its annual Christmas production of a Langston Hughes play, *Black Nativity*. This gospel-infused play also features a quilt, one that several characters are

making to give to a homeless man, and for 20 years Penumbra used a quilt made by a local pastor as the prop. But about the time Lewis made the *Gem* quilt, Penumbra decided to start a quilting circle that would produce a group quilt for *Nativity*. An invitation was put out to the community asking for volunteers to contribute three hours a weekend for three months. All who participated in making a quilt would get a free ticket to the show.

"I remember how worried we were about getting volunteers," said Lewis to another dedicated member of that circle, Gail Hanson, sitting with her at Penumbra. "I said, 'Homegirl, you and me are going to burn the midnight oil if nobody else who volunteers has sewing skills!'" Some did show up without sewing skills, Lewis recalled, "but we got them started sewing long strips for the background.

ABOVE: Dense stitches at the center of the *Gem of the Ocean* quilt, illustrating a "City of Bones." BELOW: The celebrated quilt in the theater lobby. NEXT PAGE: Examining a batch of Lewis's latest hand dyes.

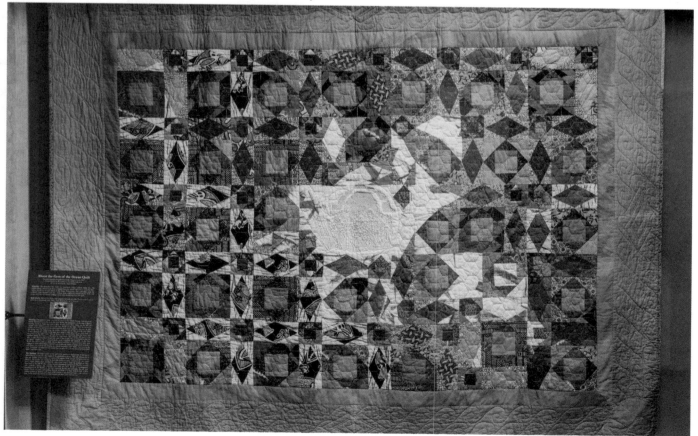

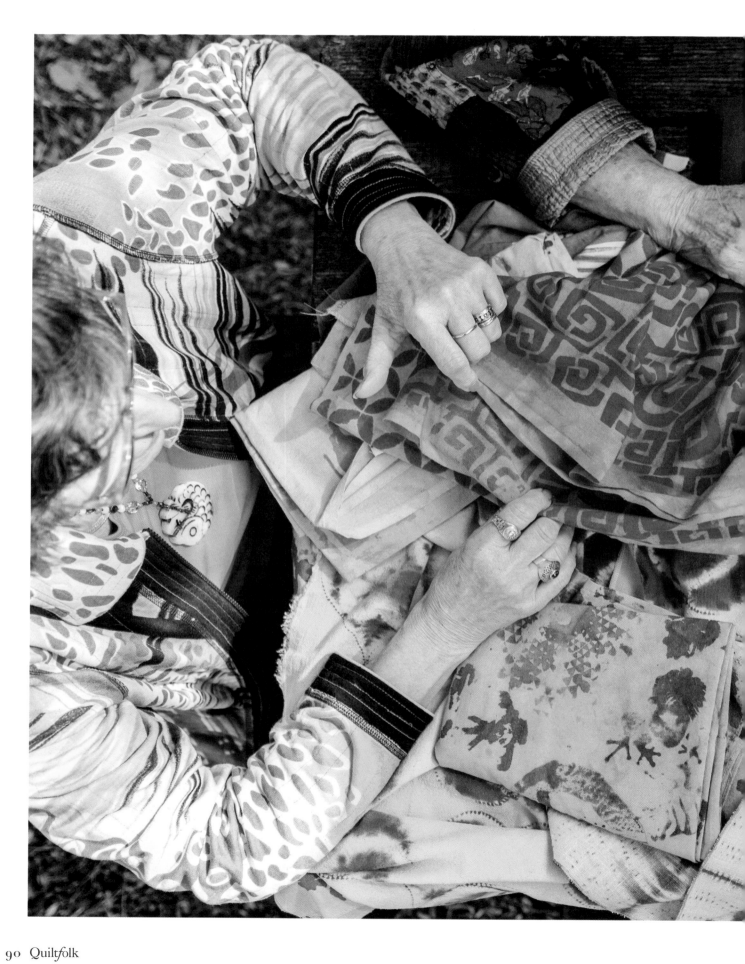

CLOCKWISE FROM UPPER LEFT: Hanson, dedicated quilter for more than 25 years; a "gem" of a theater; members of the Penumbra Quilt Circle holding a quilt they made for *Black Nativity* (L-R: Lewis, Mimie Pollard, Hanson, and Audience Services Director Anita Robinson).

Seats are ready for audience members at Minnesota's intimate Penumbra Theatre.

If they didn't sew, we got them to iron or make snacks. I loved the collaboration that we had with people of all ages and colors and experiences, and watching the camaraderie grow." For three years in a row, the Penumbra Quilt Circle worked in this way and some of the same volunteers helped each time.

The most constant quilting reference within the theater resides on its very walls. For the 30th anniversary of Penumbra, two inside walls were painted with murals that resemble rows of quilt blocks. Collectively, these honor the theater's past but also celebrate the local community and the nation's most iconic black artists and artworks. One block references the Rondo neighborhood in Saint Paul, an established African American neighborhood that was shattered by the construction of the I-94 freeway through its heart. Another square references the fact that founder Lou Bellamy, who grew up there, woke up one day at age 4 to a burning cross in the family's front yard. Other squares celebrate great artworks, including Alice Walker's novel *The Color Purple,* and artists such as Dinah Washington and Billie Holiday.

Sarah Bellamy, artistic director and daughter of Penumbra's founder, has said of the company's mission that "We are in this business not just to move audiences with great art, but to support justice, to use the unique power of theater to open hearts and minds." At Penumbra, quilts sometimes help actors amplify that power and move audiences farther than words and scenes alone.

BY **Jenni Grover**

Guilded Tapestry
TEXTILE CENTER

———————

Walk through the doors of Textile Center and you'll feel a buzz of energy. All around you, from the lively gift shop to the light-filled art galleries, from the overflowing library to the bustling classrooms, people are making and doing.

Executive Director Karl Reichert, clad in a *shibori*-dyed shirt he made, says the energy is infectious, and that's the goal of Textile Center: to inspire visitors, to promote the cross-pollination of dozens of crafts, and to teach anyone who desires to learn about fiber arts.

Textiles are ubiquitous in our lives and in our memories. Most of us know the feel of a soft handwoven blanket or the heft of an embellished gown. Every culture embraces textiles, from clothing to bed coverings to artwork. And quilts, which can keep us cozy, honor a family's history, or move us to action through artful messages, feature prominently at Textile Center.

A world of color at Textile Center. **CLOCKWISE FROM UPPER LEFT:** *No-Name Woman GuRuMaGi* by Chunghie Lee, 2013; *Oil Ikat (homage to Virgina Davis)* by Jerry Bleem, 2012; brilliant colors outside too; hand-dyed work in the gift shop.

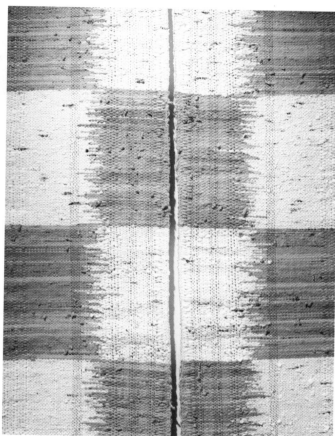

Tina Hughes, with her quilt *Too Fast: Disappearing Glaciers*, says Textile Center gives her the freedom to explore new techniques.

"Twenty-five years ago, Textile Center was a grand vision," Reichert said, "but also a grand experiment, about bringing the guilds together and being able to find a way to create a home where all are welcome." Initially volunteer-led, Textile Center today has a large staff as well as a National Artist Advisory Council of experts like quilter Dr. Carolyn L. Mazloomi.

Textile Center connects 30 affiliated member guilds, and some host their monthly meetings there; Weavers Guild of Minnesota is housed in the facility. The Textile Center Pat O'Connor Library holds about 31,000 books and periodicals; it's one of the nation's largest circulating libraries dedicated to textiles. At Textile Center, students can take classes in a wide variety of techniques including quilting, weaving, needlework, knitting, felting, dyeing, beading, and basketry.

"Textile Center attracts a huge variety of people, for different reasons," said Katherine Simon Frank, quilter and former board member. Her involvement with the organization has led to exploring new techniques. Her current works — inspired by dreams — riff on the traditional appliqué technique of broderie perse. By adding layers of imagery and texture, Frank creates quilts that evoke feelings of connection with nature.

Art quilter and past president Tina Hughes said her work is also informed by Textile Center, specifically workshops with guest teaching artists like Ilze Aviks.

Director for Artistic Advancement Tracy Krumm has been interested in textiles all her life.

"Going through [her] class just exploded things for me," said Hughes, who is passionate about surface design. She learned from Aviks how to work outside of sewing patterns and how to make monoprint fabrics. For artists like Hughes, Textile Center offers a rich dye garden packed with a variety of plants, and a dye lab with dedicated space for members to safely work with dyes and chemicals.

Tracy Krumm, director for artistic advancement, said the organization has moved beyond its initial desire to simply serve guilds, to claim its own identity as a nationally respected center for fiber art. That's due in large part to the organization's emphasis on exhibiting artists who challenge members and visitors.

When selecting shows for Textile Center, Krumm focuses on three things: inclusion, equity, and diversity. She also aims to secure artists from around the world, giving visitors a chance to connect with different cultures. A recent exhibit of Korean artist Insook Choi's work, curated by Chunhghie Lee, featured intricate embroidered *bojagi* patchworks of hemp and silk. Earlier in 2019, Wone Vang showed irreverent cross-stitch pieces that honored the needlework of her Hmong heritage. "Almost every culture has a history embedded in textiles," Krumm said. "It's a universal vocabulary. It allows me to go anywhere in the world and have something I can relate to very closely."

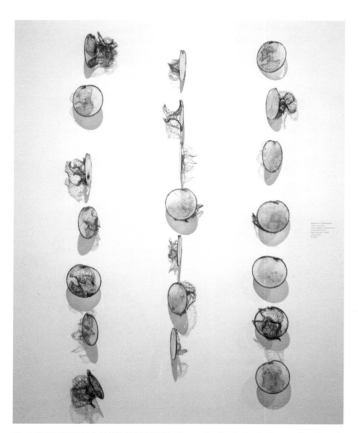

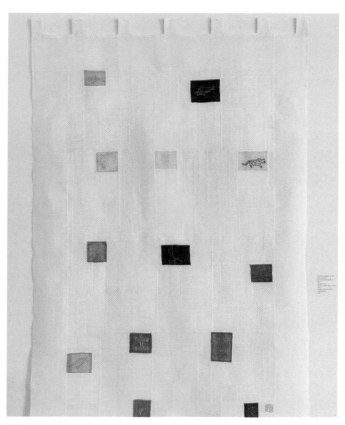

CLOCKWISE FROM UPPER LEFT: *Hyperbolic Cytoskeletons* by Carolyn Halliday, 2019; *Ramie Petroglyph Pattern Screen* by Insook Choi, 2019; textile art on display in airy galleries, including *The Color of NO* by Susan Iverson. **OPPOSITE:** *Hemp Petroglyph Pattern Patchwork Wrapping-Cloth* by Insook Choi, 2017.

Hemp Petrog
Patchwork W
2017
삼베 암각화
제작, 자연열
치자, 쑥, 황
Insook Choi
Hemp, natura
wood, cochin
seeds, indigo
yellow and b
Bojagi- hand
embroidered,
NFS

ABOVE: Katherine Simon Frank holds up her 2018 quilt, *Peter's Pick-Up Sticks*, with help from Hughes. **OPPOSITE:** Karl Reichert is Textile Center's dedicated executive director.

Textile Center may strive to inspire members with an exploration of diverse cultures from around the globe, but it's giving local kids access to art too. The Youth Fiber Art Guild is an extracurricular program for Twin Cities students elementary age and up who may not otherwise have access to fiber art programs. Teaching artists, as well as volunteers like Hughes, visit groups to teach techniques like wet felting, *kumihimo*, beading, and more. Reaching kids with fiber arts grows their curiosity and creativity.

For older kids, Textile Center offers summer internships through Step Up, a Minneapolis-based youth employment program. Interns first work at Target headquarters, shadowing product designers. Then they spend time at Textile Center learning surface design and researching textile history. Their next stop is the University of Minnesota, where they learn to design and construct garments. The internships culminate in a student fashion show at Target headquarters. Reichert says the staff and volunteers love teaching young people that they can build a lucrative career in textiles.

A hub for career artists, students, and newcomers alike, Textile Center is a simple place at heart. "There isn't any other place in the state where there's such a huge expression of textile art," said Reichert. On display near the entrance, Insook Choi's airy embroidered quilt evokes feelings of comfort and homeyness — a welcoming, even though it comes from the other side of the world.

READ A GOOD
QUILT LATELY?

Quilts and books are fast friends. Both offer comfort. Both require hours of focused creativity by their maker. And a book and a quilt both tell a story.

After 60 years in the publishing business, Lerner Books proves that Minneapolis is a place where books are born. Decades ago, a quilt was born in Minneapolis too, and that quilt has brought smiles — and business — to the publishing company ever since.

For nearly four decades, Annette Garceau was head costumer at the Guthrie Theater, a regional playhouse of national acclaim. Garceau expertly made costumes that were as memorable as she was. When she made her first quilt for a fundraiser, the quilt was classic Garceau.

Harry Lerner, founder and president of Lerner Books, was disappointed to be outbid on the magical quilt at a fundraising auction in the late 1970s. But a person with the tenacity to run a book business for six decades was not to be dissuaded: Lerner commissioned Garceau to make quilted signage for his business. Before the days of computer-made displays, vendors at trade shows used banners to identify themselves, but the banners usually weren't quilts.

Charming and imaginative, Garceau's logo quilt was appliquéd with pictorial objects representing topics of books published by Lerner, such as footballs, ships, and a guitar. Harry Lerner says conference attendees would cross the convention center just to see the quilt. Amid a sea of neon lighting and endless aisles, Garceau's work communicated precisely what quilts and books have in common: a great story.

ABOVE: Garceau's kindly quilt has been used in Lerner displays since 1978. **BELOW:** Encore! Harry Lerner (left) and associates Todd Strand and Martha Kranes present a second quilt Garceau made in 1997.

BY **Laura McDowell Hopper**

Suzanne Thao and Chuayi Yang
HMONG TEXTILES

———————

When Chuayi Yang moved to the United States at age 12, her family's focus was on her education but not on her practice of traditional *paj ntaub*, a textile art that has endured through generations of Hmong families in Southeast Asia.

Paj ntaub, pronounced "pan dau," is the Hmong word for textile and translates to "flowery cloth" in English. Known for their exquisite details, meticulous stitches, and vibrant color palettes, these textiles share countless techniques with quilting, in particular piecing and reverse appliqué.

"This is art that's been passed down for thousands of years," Yang said, "but we don't have the skills anymore." As an adult, Yang has felt this cultural loss acutely. Luckily, she comes from a long line of talented paj ntaub artists, including her mother, Suzanne Thao. Together, the two pioneered one of the most successful cultural revitalization programs at the Saint Paul-based Hmong Museum: Project Paj Ntaub.

Suzanne Thao and daughter Chuayi Yang, on the front steps of Thao's home in Saint Paul.

ABOVE: Thao works with a few pieces from an overflowing scrap basket. **OPPOSITE:** A story cloth depicts the Hmong refugee experience after the Vietnam War.

Sewing for turbulent times

When Thao was 17 years old, she was among the Hmong people who escaped from Laos after the Vietnam War in 1975. The Nong Khai refugee camp in Thailand offered Thao safety, but it did not offer her a fulfilling way to spend her days. "We had nothing to do," Thao said. "So we just made paj ntaub all day long, just to pass the time."

Originally from China, Hmong people are an ethnic minority group who settled in the mountains of Southeast Asia beginning in the early 1800s. In 1961, the Hmong were recruited by the United States Central Intelligence Agency to fight against communist expansion in Laos in a military campaign so covert it is called the Secret War. Between 1961 and 1975, an estimated 17,000 Hmong soldiers were killed and Hmong civilian casualties reached 50,000. Considered traitors by the Laotian government after the war, Hmong families fled across the treacherous Mekong River

to live in refugee camps in Thailand, before many were resettled to other countries. Minnesota was a major hub of Hmong refugee resettlement in the United States due to the state's social services, and the Hmong population grew. Today, Minnesota's Hmong population is over 65,000.

Scholars in the burgeoning field of quilt studies in the 1970s and 1980s saw paj ntaub for the first time when Hmong refugees came to the United States. Recognized as having many visual and technical connections to quilts and importance as storytelling objects, Hmong textiles were included in prominent early quilt history books. By the 1980s, Hmong sewing skills were so highly respected that Amish quilters hired Hmong textile makers to finish their quilts. Hmong women had developed their fine sewing skills generations before the Secret War and passed them down to their children at a young age.

LAOGOVIRNMEN
KAYSONE RILL.SD
HMONS NILL TRIDE BY
CHEMY AND DROPPE

ABOVE: The heart-within-a-heart motif is frequently found in the paj ntaub tradition. OPPOSITE: Hmong embroidery features vivid colors, often contrasted with solid white.

ABOVE: Thao and Yang show photographs of the matriarchs who made their respective Hmong paj ntaub sashes in the 1960s: Mee Xiong on left, Chia Lo on right. **OPPOSITE:** Chia Lo made this waist sash for daughter Thao in 1962.

Happy home

Thao learned to sew when she was 7 years old, while still in Laos. Her mother and grandmother, both considered master paj ntaub artists, taught her by candlelight in the evenings after Thao came home from school. Making paj ntaub was an important tradition and became an artistic way to share Hmong culture and history through story cloths: large textiles with pieced borders and embroidered figures that told folk tales or documented the Secret War.

Thao made fewer paj ntaub than her friends in the refugee camp because she got married, resettled with her husband to France in 1976, and focused on building a family. Thao had 4 children, including daughter Chuayi. After 14 years in France, the family moved to Minneapolis to be closer to relatives.

"Minnesota is good for me," Thao said. She loves the state's four beautiful seasons, which she says she had never experienced in Laos or France. After moving, she continued making paj ntaub for fun outside of her day job, sewing at home in the evenings like quilters around the country. She taught basic sewing skills like threading a needle and mastering beginner stitches to her children but encouraged them to focus on school.

Thao's daughter Chuayi Yang followed her mother's advice, getting a job in education after she graduated. When Yang saw a call for volunteers for a new Hmong Museum starting in the Twin Cities, she applied and became a founding board member focusing on the young museum's educational programming.

ABOVE, L-R: Sewing supplies at home; a pillow with story cloth depicting a woodland nature scene. **OPPOSITE:** In her mom's front yard, Yang holds her first-ever paj ntaub project, started at age 8.

Small stitches, big plans

The board sought to build bridges within the Hmong community. "We felt very strongly that there is an intergenerational gap," Yang said. Much of this gap is related to language loss: English-speaking grandchildren are often unable to communicate with Hmong-speaking elders. Yang thought about how her mother and grandmother had spent time together. She realized that making paj ntaub could foster these types of conversations, as it had for generations of Hmong women before — not unlike the tradition of quilting passed down through generations of American quilters.

Project Paj Ntaub was born. The next step was for Yang to find an elder to lead the ongoing small workshop series where elders teach sewing skills to younger attendees. All she needed was to remember the one paj ntaub she had made with her mother as a child to know exactly who should lead the classes: Suzanne Thao.

When Yang told her mother about Project Paj Ntaub, Thao couldn't believe it. She was skeptical and Yang finally said, "Mom, I'm serious!" Thao was ready to get started that very week. "I was so happy, I could not believe it," Thao said. "I pulled all my sewing out and planned [everything]." She wanted to begin by teaching cross-stitch (*tawmlaug* in Hmong) then move on to teaching the more complex reverse appliqué (*paj ntaub txav* in Hmong).

The classes are a combination of hands-on education and storytelling. In Project Paj Ntaub workshops, Thao sits on her favorite stool and demonstrates her work, then she turns her focus to the small group of attendees, usually adult women who, like Yang, are looking to reconnect with this sewing tradition. The workshops are kept small to encourage intimate conversations, with usually fewer than 10 people attending each event. The experience is similar to a quilting bee, with women sharing stories while they work.

ABOVE: Impossibly delicate cross-stitch work with a precious history. **OPPOSITE:** Generous host and teacher Suzanne Thao.

A home in Minnesota

Yang's appreciation for the work of her ancestors has grown, and she's seen new artists interpret paj ntaub. "Paj ntaub is an art that has evolved with people," Yang said. "Styles and designs have changed." Yang attributes this change to the storytelling element of the art. "Hmong people didn't have a written language, so their energy was poured into their paj ntaub," she said.

Project Paj Ntaub encourages students to create their own designs to tell new stories and help the tradition flourish with a new generation of artists. The basics are still there — swirling or geometric reverse appliqué with names like Snail, Ram's Horn, and Elephant's Foot, made with tiny, sometimes indiscernible stitches — but paj ntaub artists in their 20s or 30s might use hot pink instead of traditional red, or they might design new shapes and patterns rooted in the traditional work passed down to them.

Thao is a supportive teacher with her students. Her sense of humor shines in the workshops, as she cracks jokes while threading her nylon thread through needle eyes so small they are barely visible.

Thao thrives during teaching. "When somebody is doing it with you, it has meaning and purpose," she said. She also takes time to reflect while making paj ntaub. Thao feels connected through time to her ancestors when she's sewing. "I feel like I respect my grandma, I respect my mom," she said. Like many American quilters who first learned to sew from a matriarch, Thao sees paj ntaub as an art of cultural inheritance that must be taught to continue.

Project Paj Ntaub and the cultural retention work that Thao and Yang are doing have had ripple effects for both women. Yang's dedication to intergenerational relationships led her to make a recent career change: She now works at a center for Hmong elders. And Thao has found new energy through her drive to teach paj ntaub and to encourage new artists to push traditional design boundaries while learning about the past.

Like generations of quilters in America and generations of Hmong paj ntaub artists in Laos, this mother-daughter duo bridges time through sewing to ensure the future of their culture.

BY **Laura McDowell Hopper**

The Purple Ones
QUILTS FOR PRINCE

The Purple One. The Kid. The Prince of Funk. The Artist Formerly Known as Prince. His Royal Badness.

Known by many names during his nearly 40-year career, Prince Rogers Nelson revolutionized music. As one of the greatest songwriters, guitar players, and performers of his time, Prince sold over 100 million records worldwide and scored 46 hits on the Billboard Hot 100 chart with his signature blend of pop, rock, and funk.

Born and raised in Minneapolis, Prince built his career in his favorite city. After filming his landmark debut movie Purple Rain at Minneapolis's popular music venue First Avenue, Prince became a household name. He toured the world, won seven Grammy Awards and an Academy Award, and was inducted into the Rock & Roll Hall of Fame. But Minnesota remained his home, and at the height of his fame in 1987, he founded Paisley Park which served as his house and music studio in suburban Chanhassen.

After his untimely death in 2016, thousands of fans poured into the streets of Minneapolis, congregating around First Avenue, singing his songs late into the night. They hung tributes to Prince on the fence around Paisley Park. And they made quilts.

Two quilt exhibits were created in Minnesota to celebrate Prince's legacy. The annual Cherrywood Challenge chose the star as their inspiration for 2018 *(see page 148)*, and Textile Center in Minneapolis hosted an exhibit curated by quilt scholar Dr. Carolyn L. Mazloomi, which included a quilt made by Prince's own costume designer with a rainbow of hand-dyed swatches of his garments from the 1980s and 1990s.

Prince had houses around the world, but always called Minnesota home. "I like Hollywood. I just like Minneapolis a little better," he famously said. Minnesota quilters like Prince too. There are countless quilts to prove it.

New Beginnings by Devon Pfeif, winner of the Cherrywood Challenge 2018.

"*The idea of Prince performing was the first thought that came to mind when starting the Cherrywood Challenge. His fabulous music appeals to a wide variety of people. I am drawn to his R&B and his later performances. That's what I tried to capture in my portrait art quilt.*"

— DEVON PFEIF

Into the Night by Crystal Appelgate, finalist in the Cherrywood Challenge 2018.

"*Prince was daring and vivacious. He pushed the limits and was a creative force that swung on the edge of eccentricity. Each song he wrote was a carefully composed piece of art, much like the art quilts hundreds have created in his honor.*"

— CRYSTAL APPELGATE

Behind the Clouds by Eric Shumate, finalist in the Cherrywood Challenge 2018.

Quilts from Textile Center's exhibition *Commemorating His Purple Reign: A Textural Tribute to Prince*, curated and juried by Dr. Carolyn L. Mazloomi, are packed for travel; *Paisley Park Under a Cherry Moon* by Trish Williams hangs in front.

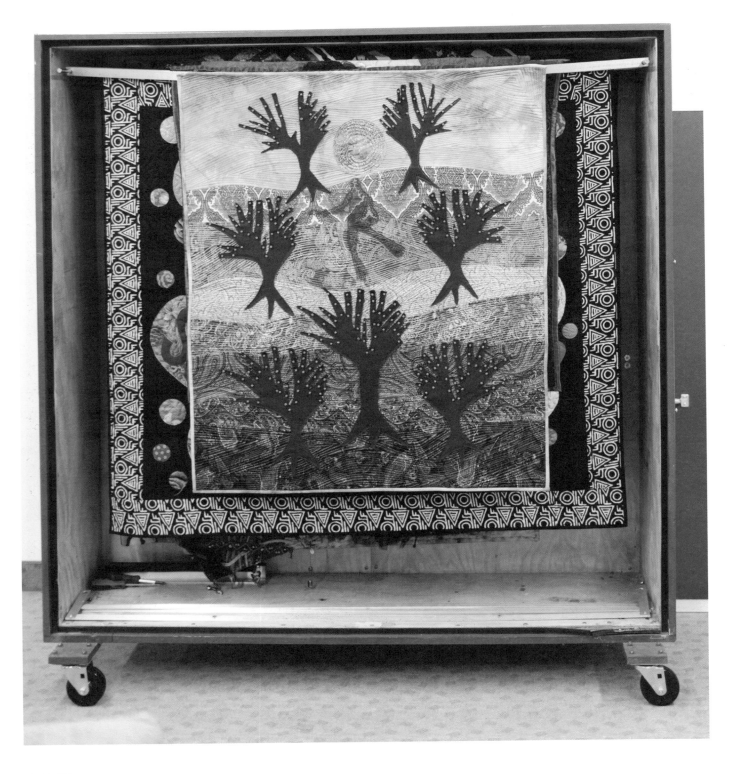

First Ave. Stardom by Heather Thormodson, finalist in the Cherrywood Challenge 2018.

"*Downtown Minneapolis was a magnet for Prince fans. First Avenue, with silver stars painted on the outside black brick, brought me out of the cow barn back home. Prince was creative, straightforward, and unafraid. That lens guides me today with my love of quilting and textile art.*"

— HEATHER THORMODSON

"Prince created a style all his own: unique, flamboyant, and ever entertaining.
It is impossible to hear his music without seeing and feeling vivid color.
My goal was to create a quilt with movement and flow, improvising with beadwork
and embroidery to reach for that unique, colorful style."

— ELLEN SMITH

Royal Riff by Ellen Smith, finalist in the Cherrywood Challenge 2018.

Fallinlove2nite by Marliss Borenz Jensen, 2016. Made with hand-dyed swatches from Prince's garments, this quilt by costume designer Jensen is part of the *Commemorating His Purple Reign* exhibition.

"His music, his flashy clothes, his provocative dance moves, and his daring attitude — everything about Prince was larger than life. The quilts in the exhibition are imaginative and pulsating with energy, and each spoke of so much love for Prince. I felt it was a fitting commemoration of a musician who made such vibrant music."

— DR. CAROLYN L. MAZLOOMI

NORTHERN STARS

Quilters Welcome

NORTHERN STARS

AN OUTSIDER MAY WONDER what there is to do all the way up in northern Minnesota. In response, a Minnesotan may smile and pat your hand before sharing with you, in the kindest, most Minnesotan way, why you should go see for yourself.

The famous Boundary Waters, a preserve of lakes and woods extending nearly 150 miles along the US border with Canada, has been called "America's most popular wilderness." Over one million acres of outdoor adventure await, and nothing beats an afternoon spent in Minnesota nature. Of course, if your idea of "camping out" means sitting and sewing for hours, that works too! Rent a cabin, set up your machine, and look out the window as you work: That water is beautiful from any angle.

You can also get a taste of rugged northern Minnesota with a journey along the North Shore region. The northeastern side of the state is studded with destination breweries, lighthouses, smokehouses, wineries, and more. In quirky Duluth, you can even find a creamery that serves vegan ice cream.

The Minnesota state of mind — relaxed, neighborly, hardy — is easy to slip into when you're up north. You might even find yourself smiling and patting people on the hand.

BY **Jenni Grover**

Do the Hardest Thing

KAREN McTAVISH

A fresh breeze is blowing through Karen McTavish's Duluth apartment, and sunshine bathes the cozy sofa where she sits. On her lap is a quilt she's calling a "collaboration." When fellow quilter Grace Forsythe passed away, McTavish inherited a stack of her blocks and fabric. McTavish is fashioning them into a quilt packed with personality, including a hand-stitched and improvised floral appliqué border.

Like many things McTavish makes, the quilt honors tradition while still feeling fresh and contemporary. It's her signature move: Learn a classic quilting style and its history, apply current techniques to execute it, and create something timeless.

McTavish, a Minneapolis native, has a big personality. Her voice is strong and bold; she speaks with equal measures of frankness and vulnerability. She's got tattoos and listens to loud metal music while quilting. And like so many of us, she's faced some tough times and relied on quilting to get through them.

A true original, Karen McTavish knows all quilts begin with a needle and thread.

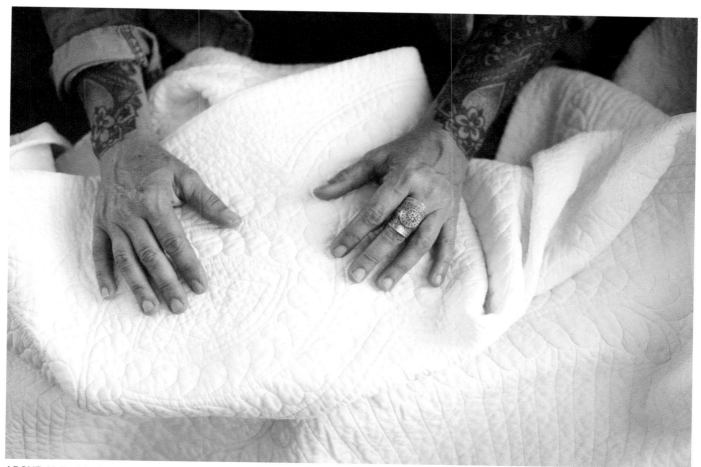

ABOVE: McTavish sits with a whole-cloth white-work quilt made in 2001. **OPPOSITE:** Her free-motion quilting style and fierce faith in the talent of others have earned McTavish a devoted following.

Her name as a verb

McTavish has been a professional longarm quilter since 1997 and a teacher since 2001. Her work has earned her appearances on networks like PBS and HGTV, and she's published seven books. Students travel from around the world for classes at McTavish Quilting Studio, and Minnesota Quilters Inc. named her Quilter of the Year in 2017.

But she might be best known for inventing a freehand background filler that quilters use as an alternative to stippling (free-motion quilting in tight meandering curves). Her technique creates a flowing texture like rippling water or a soft wind; it resembles the style of Alphonse Mucha, an art nouveau painter from whose work McTavish draws inspiration. She dubbed her technique "Cartoon Wonder Woman Hair," but as more and more quilters adopted the style, it became "McTavishing."

In 2005, she published *Mastering the Art of McTavishing*. But she's "100% uncomfortable" with the fact hat she became a brand name for the quilting technique. "I never really wanted ownership of it," she said. "It's so widely used now. Everybody does it differently." In her book, McTavish calls the method her "fingerprint." She explains that every quilter who tries it will develop their unique interpretation and should feel empowered to own it. "I recommend naming your signature quilting style after yourself by adding an "-ing" to your last name. That way it's always your personal style."

McTavish is modest about many of her other accomplishments too. She's won numerous awards over the years but said the one that matters most is a Faculty Choice ribbon Linda V. Taylor gave her at the Minnesota Quilters' Show in 1999. "It made me feel bona fide," McTavish said.

In 2014, McTavish used a Zen Chic pattern to piece and sew *Cross It*.

Going her own way

That was just two years after McTavish moved to Duluth with a dream of making it as a longarm quilter. A single mom at the time of the move (daughter Ally, now 30, was in third grade back then), McTavish had no experience, but she did have assurances that longarming was an achievable career.

McTavish devoted every waking minute to researching the craft and getting comfortable with her machine. At the time, pantograph quilting (using a paper stencil to create an all-over pattern) was the fashion, but she didn't feel at ease working from the back of the machine. "I started from the front, using hand-quilting stencils, trying to follow along what a hand quilter would have done," she said. "I almost looked at the machine like a pencil, and it felt really comfortable." She researched older quilting techniques at the library, reading books and learning traditional styles she could replicate by machine.

But she faced resistance when it came time to negotiate fair fees for her work. "People were clutching their pearls over paying anything more than $100 for a quilt," she said. "I was below the

McTavish made this striking painting on black fabric in 2015, a tumultuous year in which she went through a divorce and opened her quilting studio.

poverty line the first two years." Hand quilting was still the preferred method locally; some folks didn't think machine quilting was respectable. And clients who *did* want machine quilting expected pantograph quilting (at pantograph prices). They had never encountered custom heirloom machine quilting, which takes much longer.

Looking back, McTavish admits that she didn't know how to communicate the intricacies of her craft to those early clients — and they didn't quite know what to expect from her. She defied the norm,

not just with her new technique, but also with her youth. She suspects that her dreadlocks, tattoos, and piercings didn't help. "I would just pray for gray hair, because that gives you credibility," she said.

As it does for so many entrepreneurs, her path felt lonely. "Being isolated for the first four years was really scary and hard, but it was actually a good time for me to learn my own style," she said, recalling 15-hour workdays. Whenever she quilted, she asked herself: What would a hand quilter do? She never chose the easy path nor took shortcuts.

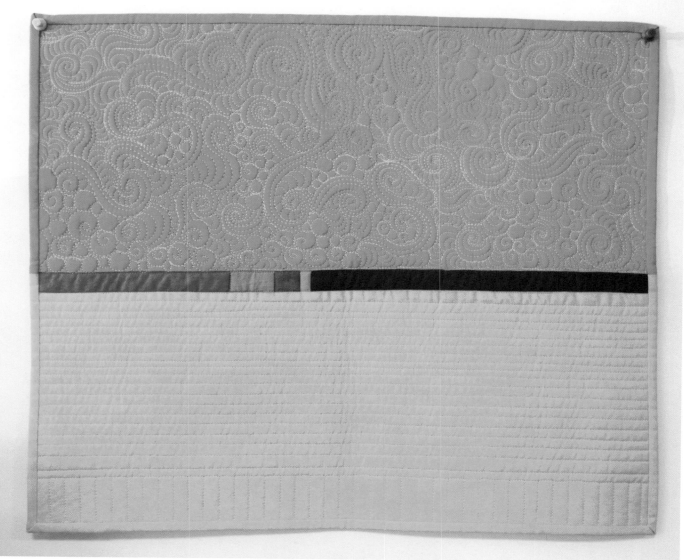

ABOVE: *Horizon*, designed and pieced by Cheryl Dennison and quilted by McTavish. **OPPOSITE:** McTavish, standing with longarm quilter, instructor, and friend Dennison, a full-time employee at McTavish Quilting Studio from the start.

Decades of friendship and art

In those early years, McTavish found support among local artists. Her first residence in Duluth was Washington Studios Artist Cooperative, a live-work space in a converted junior high school. Modern quilter Cheryl Dennison was on the panel that accepted McTavish's application to the co-op and they became fast friends.

Today Dennison fills a number of roles at McTavish Quilting Studio. She's a master at computerized quilting and makes many of the samples that decorate the studio walls. "I like to break rules,"

Dennison said, a trait she and McTavish clearly share.

Dennison also fills a vital role in community building. At the time of *Quiltfolk*'s visit, Dennison was undergoing treatment for breast and lung cancer and had to reduce her workload temporarily. But she has hosted sew-ins for fellow cancer patients at the studio. "Those gals will hang out with Cheryl and work and talk and laugh and swear," said McTavish. Fostering community for those quilters is important, she added, because sickness can breed isolation.

 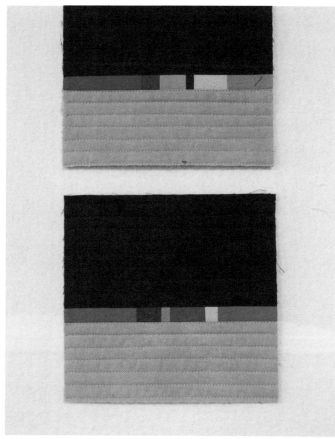

ABOVE, L-R: Extra work space on the top of treadle machines; two unbound pieces from Dennison's *Horizons* series. **OPPOSITE:** McTavish in her wheelhouse.

Passion for instruction

Today, McTavish prioritizes teaching people to build successful quilting businesses. Her motivation is personal: She is once again a single mom, to 14-year-old son Storm after a divorce.

"My passion is making sure that somebody can invest in these machines and make a living at what they do," she said. She doesn't want anyone to feel trapped into making unhealthy compromises to stay afloat. Her mission has become "helping women be self-sufficient, raise kids, and have a roof over their heads, without needing a second income."

McTavish has fought hard to be strong on her own. Quilting is the easy part, she explained, but the business side can be brutal. When she started, she worked long hours and found professional advice hard to come by. Today, she gives liberally of her knowledge and experience.

"The reason why quilting is such a frugal industry is that women have a hard time charging what they're worth," said McTavish. When she teaches, she devotes plenty of time to reinforcing the value of quilting. She draws an analogy between quilters and auto mechanics: Both require years of training and operate shops packed with expensive machinery and tools, so why shouldn't quilters charge comparable fees?

ABOVE: Customer Kimberly Swink sees for the first time a quilt made with her late daughter's clothing. **OPPOSITE:** A bowl of bobbins holds limitless potential.

Good medicine

On the day *Quiltfolk* visited McTavish, one of her clients, Kimberly Swink, a longarm quilter in West Sparta, NY, dropped in to pick up a commemorative quilt honoring the passing of her daughter Francesca in 2018. From three laundry baskets of Francesca's clothes, McTavish and her staff created a spectacular quilt that includes tie-dyed t-shirts made by Francesca. "They did a perfect job," said Swink, hugging McTavish.

Creating projects that are beautiful and useful feeds her spirit, McTavish said. "It's a huge responsibility to keep a loved one warm." To deal with loss and other difficult emotions, she often turns to hand sewing. McTavish recently lost her black lab mix rescue dog, Rudy, and right now, sewing feels like healing. Each stitch, she explained, "feels like moving forward, onward, getting through whatever pain and suffering you're going through."

Today, McTavish has the stylish gray hair she once prayed for and the peace of mind that comes from running a rock-solid business that creates joy for so many. She plans to never retire. Instead she'll keep breaking rules and teaching other quilters to claim their space and livelihood. *Qf*

BY **Laura McDowell Hopper**

Quilted Harmonies
SCOTT LUNT

When Scott Lunt isn't quilting, he might be found playing the guitar in his cozy A-frame house with a view of Duluth. As a musician, radio DJ, and founder of a local music festival, Lunt makes quilts mostly about music. His interpretations, like a good song cover, help bring music to life in new ways.

Lunt became a serious quilter in 2015 and sees parallels between quilting and the music world he's known for decades. The way musicians come together in a band to create something harmonious is, to Lunt, similar to the way different fabrics form a quilt. The parallels don't stop there: As a DJ, he's "piecing together a bunch of different songs into a theme." Lunt's musical life seamlessly translates into quilts.

Scott Lunt at home, playing the 1972 Gibson guitar he inherited from his grandfather.

Dog Ady loves to nap on a Grandmother's Flower Garden quilt made by Lunt's mother in 1992.

Lunt has known quilts since childhood; his mother is a quilter. In his 20s, he made a baby quilt for a friend then crafted a quilt out of his old Boy Scout and paramedic uniforms. He thought of those quilts as one-offs, until he met fellow Duluth resident Karen McTavish who helped "rekindle" his interest in quilting. Lunt took a class with the legendary quilter then developed his skills with patterns and eventually started creating his own designs.

For Lunt, making quilts about music has been intuitive. He had toyed with the idea of creating embroidered reproductions of favorite album covers, like Joy Division's seminal 1979 album *Unknown Pleasures*. As Lunt's focus changed to quilts, he decided to use the record's stark black background and iconic white peaks to fashion a high-contrast quilt using bias tape to create the lines, instead of embroidery.

Lunt then began making quilts about bands he enjoys, like Duluth-based indie band Low, known for their trance-like tempos and sparse arrangements. Lunt interpreted Low's song "Violence" with improvised piecing of denim mimicking waves and yellow appliquéd song lyrics. After years traveling the world with Low, Lunt feels a special connection to the band, who bought the quilt from him.

Recently, Lunt attended QuiltCon in Nashville where he admired the modern quilts in the show and took in the sights and sounds of Music City. At a concert, he heard folk singer Mary Gauthier sing "Mercy Now." The song's message of hope and kindness resonated with Lunt, who bought thrifted fabrics in Nashville to create a quilt emblazoned with the song's title.

CLOCKWISE FROM UPPER LEFT: Self-portrait *Starfire*, 2018; the quilter pondering his next project; Morse code in *Quilts Are Magic* and, in lower right, Lunt's song-inspired *Mercy Now*.

This double-knit patchwork was just a top when Lunt found it on eBay; he finished his *Orphan Quilt* this year.

ABOVE: Detail, *Camp Quilt*. OPPOSITE: Using denim and patches collected from his travels, Lunt hand quilts outdoorsy words into *Camp Quilt*.

Lunt had a quilt juried into QuiltCon, and he collaborated with Duluth quilters to organize small gallery shows, which led to his first solo exhibit, *Quilts Are Magic*. Lunt sold four quilts during the run of his show, including a quilt based on one of singer-songwriter Gram Parsons's famous white suits.

As Lunt has found his voice in quilts, his taste has evolved. Precision is not his style: "too Martha Stewart-y." He finds quilts made without patterns, "like Sherri Lynn Wood's quilts or Gee's Bend

quilts," to have more character. There's a push and pull between Lunt's appreciation of meticulously made quilts and his desire for the creative abandon of improvised quilting.

Lunt plans to continue making quilts about music, while also stretching himself as an improv quilter and experimenting with unusual materials, like a canvas tent he just purchased. Whatever the material may be, Scott Lunt's stitches come together like notes in a song to create melodious quilts. *Qf*

BY **Jenni Grover**

Up to the Challenge

CHERRYWOOD HAND DYED FABRICS

Karla Overland is trying to decide what color to dye her hair. The owner of Cherrywood Hand Dyed Fabrics usually matches her hair to the company's annual quilting challenge. When we met at her offices in Brainerd, Minnesota, she still sported a shock of purple in honor of 2018's Prince-themed challenge. But 2019's Bob Ross theme was proving tough because it includes not one but eight colors.

Cherrywood fabrics have long been a favorite of quilters, but the company's annual challenges have introduced the hand-dyed fabrics to a broader audience since Overland launched the competition in 2014. Hundreds of quilters participate annually, and the resulting mini quilts travel to shows around the world. In April 2020, the Prince exhibit will be on display in Chanhassen, home of Prince's Paisley Park.

The yearly challenges are just one way Overland honors the enduring color sensibility of Cherrywood while ensuring the company serves contemporary quilters too.

Karla Overland examines *Colors of the World*; at her right lies the luxurious *Cherry Roll Vine*.

A photograph of the late Dawn Hall, Cherrywood founder and vibrant visionary.

Overland met Cherrywood founder Dawn Hall in the late 1990s through the Pinetree Patchworkers Quilt Guild and started working for her in 2000. Hall, who founded Cherrywood Hand Dyed Fabrics in 1987, had already been fighting ovarian cancer for about three years. She mentored Overland, sharing secret color recipes and preparing her to take over the small business.

When Hall died in 2002, Overland committed herself to strengthening and growing the business. "She was a quiet, shy woman, who just let the fabric speak for itself," she said about Hall. Today, Cherrywood sells 325 colors of hand-dyed fabrics to customers around the world, totaling about 28,000 yards annually. It's a long way from Hall's start, dyeing fabric in her own house.

Overland keeps swatches of every color that Cherrywood Hand Dyed Fabrics has ever offered, each with a recipe, many drawn in Hall's careful handwriting. Once known for producing muted colors, the company has evolved. "If you look at the palette over the years, it's lightened up, brightened up," said Overland. "The modern quilt movement was a huge influence on that."

The company's fabrics are offered in pretty bundles of color gradations (four, eight, or 12 steps), with names like "Kiwi Berry," "Alaskan Sunset," and "Forest Floor." When she speaks about her colors, Overland says she "tends to" them, as though they're living plants in a wild garden. They are "organic," she

Going for a dip: Overland soaks a length of muslin to test a shade she's calling "Grass Green."

explains, and change all the time, requiring constant recipe tweaks. Factors like water temperature and quality, a new tub of Procion dye, or even her mood can impact the final color of the fabric.

Overland instituted a few processes that help keep things consistent. The blenders she uses to mix dye are numbered one to eight, as are the rows of washing machines used to dye fabric. And she tells her staff, "When you see me in my dye shirt, don't talk to me. It takes a lot of concentration."

Still, perfection is far from possible and the company ends up with batches of fabric that are lovely but not quite right. Overland's team chops them up for multi-colored grab bags that are as pretty as confetti. There's no waste in the operation; even strings obtained from washing fabric are bagged and sold to quilters who use them as decorative elements. Nearly every aspect of her process is purposeful, and she's dedicated to reusing its byproducts — even lint. "Nobody's lint is as pretty as ours," she said.

The fabric's creamy suede-like texture must also be consistent so quilters cutting into yardage end up with similar-looking pieces that have only subtle variations. To avoid bunching and twisting in the machines, fabric is dyed in two-yard pieces; the process includes multiple rounds of washing, dyeing, and rinsing.

FROM LEFT: Powdered dye is carefully measured to create consistent colors; green is good; Overland says Cherrywood has been "baking" their own dye formulas for over 30 years.

ABOVE: A vintage dye display, still useful after all these years. **OPPOSITE:** Detail of *Passage*, pieced using gradations of Cherrywood's "Kiwi Berry."

Overland employs five women who work from home to finish the fabric. Her "manglers" use large mangle laundry machines that simultaneously roll, press, and dry the fabric, which they then cut and package, inspecting every inch along the way. The final product is preshrunk, with a high thread count and a soft, fuzzy texture that has been touched by hands 10 to 15 times.

Overland's passion for handwork is evident not only in Cherrywood fabrics, but also in the decor that surrounds her and her staff. In the hall near Overland's office hangs a pineapple quilt from the 1880s, foundation-pieced by hand in suit-weight wool in deep shades of oxblood red, burgundy, black, and charcoal. The colors are richly textured, reminding her of Cherrywood fabrics.

The quilt's countless hours of handwork resonate with her too. Overland takes pride in hard work and in the fact that, for 32 years, Cherrywood has been woman-owned and -operated. She remembers marveling, back in college, that a sustainable career in textiles might be possible. Today, she treasures her role as not only owner, but also designer and colorist, giving quilters hundreds of creative possibilities.

Now if she could just choose a color to dye her hair.

Quilt by Samuel Isaac Myers, circa 1930, Park Rapids, Minnesota. Collection of the Minnesota Historical Society, Saint Paul, Minnesota.

Quilt by Samuel Myers

BY **Linda McShannock**

Samuel Isaac Myers (1874–1935) of Park Rapids, Minnesota, and his father Thomas constructed the park buildings at Itasca State Park, including the well-known Douglas Lodge, the oldest surviving building in the Minnesota state park system. Besides buildings, the multitalented Myers produced intricate india-ink maps and detailed architectural plans. He completed oil paintings of Itasca State Park, wrote songs and poetry, and played several musical instruments. Myers also translated his paintings into quilts.

This appliquéd and embroidered quilt made circa 1930 by Myers now belongs to the Minnesota Historical Society (MNHS). The MNHS collection holds few quilts made by men (two of Myers's quilts are in the MNHS collection, along with two of his ink maps), and very few quilts are artist-rendered landscapes. It seems natural that Minnesota, known as the Land of 10,000 Lakes, should have a quilt that includes a scenic "up north" Minnesota lake depiction.

Myers's dream-like, pastel quilt illustrates a sunset reflected in one of the many lakes within Itasca State Park boundaries. Part of the scene includes a romanticized image of an Indigenous camp. The quilt conveys a sense of isolation with the lone camp surrounded by the grandiose natural landscape.

The quilt is painterly in its composition. Tall pine trees stand behind the camp scene and line the white sand beach. The forest, setting sun, water, and paths are made from a careful selection of printed fabrics which feature surface embroidery to provide texture and further detail. Running stitches create waves and reflection across the water. Spot stitches create texture on the leaves and suggest rocks along the shore.

This pictorial image is framed with rays of printed cottons, proving the popularity of the Dresden Plate pattern. Many of the entries to the 1933 Sears National Quilt Contest for the Century of Progress exhibition in Chicago included non-traditional subjects and fueled an interest in quiltmaking. The subdued color palette in Myers's quilt is typical of the 1930s when improved technology within the textile industry resulted in new colors. Local feed stores began selling feed bags made with popular prints for homemakers to reuse. Such prints may have been available at the Park Rapids feed store.

Even so, during the Great Depression, resources were scarce for rural families like the Myerses. In a 1935 letter to his brother, Myers asked for "two dollars for firewood to warm the house." The quilt does have a thick batting and is well used. Winters were long and construction projects lagged, giving him time for craftwork.

We do not know what motivated Myers to construct his quilts. Quilting in winter might have been a better choice than oil paints in an enclosed space with four small children underfoot. But Myers was ill for many years and possibly housebound. Perhaps, like many quilters, he found the quilting process therapeutic. As for the subject, Minnesotans never tire of reflecting on those summer landscapes. *QF*

Quiltfolk is proud to collaborate with the American Quilt Study Group (AQSG) on this Trunk Show, an intimate look at one extraordinary quilt. *For more information on AQSG's mission, visit americanquiltstudygroup.org.*

ON THE CUTTING TABLE

As we wrap up Issue 13, so many of the wonderful images
we captured did not make it into the featured stories.
Here are just a few of our favorites. Thank you to everyone who
shared their stories and spaces with us.